Jesse and Frank James:
THE FAMILY HISTORY

Jesse Woodson James in Confederate guerrilla uniform. Photo made at Platte City, Missouri in 1864 when Jesse was sixteen years of age. (Photo courtesy of the James Farm.)

Jesse and Frank James:
THE FAMILY HISTORY

By PHILLIP W. STEELE

PELICAN PUBLISHING COMPANY
GRETNA 1994

First printing , June 1987
Second printing, January 1989
Third printing, January 1991
Fourth printing, March 1994

Library of Congress Cataloging-in-Publication Data

Steele, Phillip W.
    Jesse and Frank James: the family history.

    Bibliography: p.
    Includes index.
    1. James family. 2. James, Jesse, 1847-1882—
Family. 3. James, Frank, 1844-1915—Family. 4. West
(U.S.)—Biography. I. Title.
CT274.J35S74   1987   929′.2′0973   87-8524
ISBN: 0-88289-653-9

*Cover photo of Jesse and Frank James courtesy of Joe
Ann Byland of Carrollton, Illinois, and Sandra
Reynolds Ogg of Brighton, Illinois.*

Manufactured in the United States of America

Published by Pelican Publishing Company, Inc.
1101 Monroe Street, Gretna Louisiana 70053

Contents

Alexander Franklin (Frank) James, around age 21. (Photo courtesy of the James Farm.)

Acknowledgments

Acknowledging all the sources necessary to make this James family history would be impossible. Hundreds of family researchers and fellow James historians have contributed. This writer, as well as the thousands of future James researchers, owes a tremendous debt of gratitude for the assistance of those who have made this study possible. Sources that have been especially helpful are as follows:

Lawrence H. Barr, Jesse James's grandson,
Overland Park, Kansas

Thelma Duncan Barr,
Overland Park, Kansas

James R. Ross, Jesse James's great-grandson,
Santa Ana, California

Milton F. Perry, Superintendent,
Clay County Parks and Historic Sites and
Curator, James Farm,
Kearney, Missouri

The James Farm—
Staff and Family Research Records,
Kearney, Missouri

Friends of the James Farm—
Board of Directors

7

Dr. William A. Settle,
author of *Jesse James Was His Name*
Carl W. Breihan,
author of *The Man Who Shot Jesse James*
Kentucky Historical Society,
Frankfort, Kentucky
Ted Yeatman,
Nashville, Tennessee
Steve Eng,
Nashville, Tennessee
National Outlaw and Lawmen History Association
Western Research Center, University of Wyoming,
Laramie, Wyoming
Forks of Elkhorn Church History, Kentucky
James Coleman James,
Old Hickory, Tennessee
Wynne James III,
Bethesda, Maryland
Wanda James Ryan,
Kokomo, Indiana
Peggy Woods,
Orosi, California
Diana Faber,
Brewster, Kansas
Claudia Wagoner,
Fayetteville, Arkansas
Mrs. Arnold C. Franklin, Jr.,
Brooksville, Florida
Charles Luton,
Danville, Illinois
Frank James,
McEwen, Tennessee
Dr. and Mrs. Till Huston,
Athens, Georgia

Alva Lester Burden,
Tecumseh, Oklahoma
Rick Burden,
Prairie Grove, Arkansas
Georgia Hall,
Logandale, Nevada
H. L. Griffey,
Kearney, Missouri
Dale Samuel,
Sparta, Kentucky
Bill Stamper,
Springdale, Arkansas
Iona Vaughan,
Clifty, Arkansas
Clifford Samuel,
Springdale, Arkansas
Maisie Mobley,
Prairie Grove, Arkansas
Joan M. Beamis, William E. Pullen,
authors of *Background of a Bandit*
Kelley Louise,
author of *Wichita County Beginnings*
Jack Loftin,
author of *Trails Through Archer County*
Ruth E. Reuther,
author of *A Century of Faithful Witness*
Dr. J. R. Reuther,
Wichita Falls, Texas
Marley Brant,
Burbank, California
Barry Roland Weaver,
author of "Jesse James in Arkansas"
Pam Banner,
James Farm Staff

Mary Susan and Jesse Edwards James, children of Jesse Woodson and Zerelda Mimms James. (Photo courtesy of the James Farm.)

Jesse and Frank James:
THE FAMILY HISTORY

Zerelda James Samuel, mother of Jesse, Frank, and Susan James. The black hand band she is wearing signifies her mourning over Jesse's death. Her right arm, which was blown away by the Pinkerton's flare explosion in her home, is covered. (Photo courtesy of the James family.)

Introduction

Most people would agree that over the past century Jesse and Frank James have retained their position as America's greatest folk heroes, and this position will likely continue unchallenged for years to come. Folk heroes exist in all nations, societies, and cultures, although these honored personalities do not always merit the distinction bestowed. Often, folk heroes are created to fill a social need. Such social need may have contributed to the James legend.

Born along the Missouri-Kansas border, these sons of a Baptist minister experienced armed conflict, political turmoil, and deprivation at an early age. Their legend no doubt had its beginning during the Civil War, as a result of their participation with Confederate guerrilla forces and the respect such border ruffians earned among Southern sympathizers. The deprivation and degradation experienced by Southern sympathizers during the post-war period also greatly contributed to the James brothers' becoming outlaws. Their daring exploits, including the nation's first daylight bank robbery and their train robbery, often were directed against enterprises that were owned or controlled by Northern interests. Southern sym-

13

Thema Duncan Barr, wife of Jesse James's grandson, Lawrence Barr, discusses family history at the 1983 James family reunion on the James Farm in Kearney, Missouri. (Photo by author.)

The James home as it appears today.

pathizers, humiliated by defeat and post-war injustice, considered the James brothers' crimes as a justifiable continuation of the Civil War.

Although no proof exists to support the legend, Robin Hood-type tales of Jesse and Frank robbing the rich to give to the poor were invented. The impoverished Southerners and those throughout the nation who were critical of banks and railroads embraced these legends, and public sentiment made the James brothers martyrs to their cause, no doubt contributing to their successful evasion of the law for some seventeen years. Although rewards were offered totalling as much as $50,000, Jesse and Frank James were never captured. Jesse's career ended when he was assassinated by his associate, Bob Ford, in 1882 and Frank's when he voluntarily surrendered to the Missouri governor, Thomas Crittenden, a few months later.

Several respected, nonfiction accounts of the Jameses' history have been published over the years. Far outnumbering these respected authors, however, numerous pulp writers have chosen to use Jesse and Frank James as central characters in fictional, dime novels. Such writers of "historical" fantasy found that the use of the James brothers' name was magic to assure fast sales, and this phenomenon still continues to some extent. During a 1983 James family reunion Lawrence Barr, Jesse James's grandson, was asked about the magic of his grandfather's name in American literature, and he commented, "You can sell anything with Jesse or Frank James's name on it. Here in Kearney, Missouri, the best restaurant in town even features a Frank James hamburger."

The numerous fictional books and articles written over the years have been confused with history, making it difficult for the serious historian to separate fact from folklore. William A. Settle, author of *Jesse James Was His Name,* (one of the most respected and authoritative accounts of the lives of Jesse and Frank James), explains, "Fact and fiction are so intertwined that it is difficult—at times impossible—to untangle them."

Frank James himself apparently found these fictional accounts a matter of concern. In a letter to a friend he wrote, "I found one of those cheap novels about me and Jesse. There is no truth in them, and they should not be sold to young boys of today. We will not let our son Robbie read them. The one I found was about us robbing a train. It is sickening to read how Dingus [a nickname for Jesse James] bragged about what he had done. I never heard Jess ever brag about who he was or what he did. A lot of robberies blamed on us we never did."

Legend and folklore have generated within American families a desire for reflected glory, and today it has become quite popular to claim a relationship to the James brothers. The James family home near Kearney, Missouri has been completely restored and is operated as a major Missouri tourist attraction by Clay County, Missouri Department of Parks, Recreation, and Historic Sites. Each year hundreds of visitors seek to prove a family connection with the James brothers. Most claims are based on a hapless comment by "grandmother" to the effect that the family is "kin" to Jesse and Frank James. Usually, these grandmothers have conveniently died before elaborating on this claim to their descendants.

A relationship with the James brothers has become so important that on at least two occasions families have even resorted to alleging illegitimacy to validate their claims. A lady in Hot Springs, Arkansas, whom

Alexander Franklin (Frank) James after his acquittals. (Photo courtesy of the James Farm.)

Milton Perry, left, curator of the James Farm and Museum; James R. Ross, great grandson of Jesse James; and Dr. William A. Settle, James historian, all assisted author Phillip W. Steele, right, in this family history of Jesse and Frank James.

this writer interviewed, has reason to believe her grandmother was an illegitimate daughter of Frank James. After his acquittal Frank spent several months in Hot Springs as a horse race starter and operator of a Wild West show in the Happy Hollow Amusement Park. During this period Frank supposedly had an affair which resulted in the illegitimate birth. The only proof was vague comments made by the grandmother but not fully explained before she died.

Similarly, a Kansas man reports he overheard a conversation between his father and uncle when he was a child that leads him to believe his father was an illegitimate son of Jesse James. It seems that after their unsuccessful bank robbery attempt in Northfield, Minnesota, Jesse and Frank hid for a few days in a Missouri blacksmith's barn. The blacksmith's daughter carried food to the outlaws and became intimate with Jesse during their stay. Nine months later the girl's illegitimate son was born. Such claims based on overheard conversations from the past further point out the popularity today of being a relative of the James brothers.

It is this desire by so many to establish a family connection with the Jameses that has prompted this writer to pursue their family history. Although this family history was originally outlined most creditably in the book *Background of a Bandit* by Joan Beamis and William Pullen (1971[1]; 1981[2]) a great amount of additional family material has been found since.

Sold to Clay County, Missouri in 1978 by Lawrence, Forster, and Chester Barr, grandsons of Jesse James, the James farm has not only become a tourist attraction but also serves as a museum and James research center. The Friends of the James Farm organization consists of James history buffs from around the world. This group is also headquartered at the James Farm and sponsors James family reunions and history conferences on the farm. Milton Perry, Superintendent of Clay County, Missouri Division of Historic Sites, also serves as curator of the James Farm and Museum as well as secretary of the Friends organization. The family history collected by the Farm from the many visitors and relatives attending the annual reunions and made available by Milton Perry has greatly contributed to this project. Lawrence Barr also contributed his family records before his death in 1984, and his wife, Thelma Duncan Barr, has been of tremendous assistance in documenting James family

Jesse Woodson James. This photo is believed to have been made in Nebraska City, Nebraska and sent by Jesse to his mother, Zerelda Samuel.

A rare photo of Judge James Ross, great grandson of Jesse James; and his great uncle, Lawrence Barr, Mary Susan James's son. (Photo taken at a James family reunion by Dr. William A. Settle, a noted James author.)

records. James Ross, a California superior court judge and grandson of Jesse Edwards James, the only son of Jesse Woodson James, has also generously aided in the preparation of this history. This writer deeply appreciates the assistance from these researchers and James family members in the attempt to record here the most complete family history currently possible on the James family.

It is virtually impossible for any writer on family history to claim his work to be error-free, and this writer would not make such a claim. However, it is felt that the information presented here is the most complete and accurate history of Jesse and Frank James's family to date. As with any family research, writing such a history is a never-ending process—much information is still unknown. It is hoped that the information recorded here will be of assistance both to researchers and to those who have a legitimate relationship to the James family. Others, who may find that this research discredits their claim to relationship with the James family, should not be disappointed. Tales of family relationships and incidents, whether proven legitimate or not, have their own importance as American folklore and deserve to be preserved. The purpose and focus of this study, however, is to recognize the importance of documenting factual history of the James family and to provide a manual that, hopefully, will assist in separating James folklore from history for future James family researchers.

Although hundreds of James descendants can be traced to cousins of Jesse and Frank James and to their half-brothers and -sisters, the Samuels, no direct descendant of Jesse or Frank James bearing the James name remains. Frank's only son, Robert James, died childless in 1959. Jesse James's only son, Jesse Edwards, had only female offspring, all of whom married.

CHAPTER 1

The
James
Family

WILLIAM JAMES

William James, believed to have been born in 1754 in Pembrokeshire, Wales, came to America with his family at an early age.[1] Originally settling lands in Montgomery County, Pennsylvania, he later moved to Virginia, where he settled near Lickinghole Creek in Goochland County. Records indicate that William also owned land in nearby Fluvanna and Louisa counties. It was there he was married, on July 15, 1774, to Mary Hines, who was English-born. Rev. William Douglas of Saint James Northern Parish performed the ceremony in Hanover County. William died in 1805. William and Mary had the following children:

John James
    Born: 1775
    Died: 1827
    Married: Mary "Polly" Poor, March 26, 1807

1. A Tennessee James family indicates William was the son of John James and that William's brother, Thomas, founded the Tennessee James line.

Nancy Ann James
  Born: February 24, 1777
  Married: David Hodges, December 21, 1799

Mary James
  Married: Edward Lee, December 22, 1796

William James, Jr.
  Born: April 27, 1782
  Died: 1807

Richard James
  Married: Mary G. Poor, December 18, 1813

Thomas James
  Born: December 14, 1783
  Married: Mary B. Davis, September 3, 1834

Martin James
  Born: 1789
  Died: 1867
  Married: Elizabeth Key, November 21, 1825

JOHN JAMES

The lineage of Jesse and Frank James continues with John and Polly Poor James, paternal grandparents to the famous brothers. Mary "Polly" Poor, born in 1790, was the daughter of Robert Poor and Elizabeth Mims, also of Goochland County, Virginia. The Mims name here is significant, as will be pointed out later. John James was a farmer and minister.

John and Polly James left Virginia in 1811 and settled lands in Logan County, Kentucky, along Big

Zerelda James Samuel standing by her son Jesse's original gravesite on the lawn of the James farm.

Jesse James family; Zerelda (Zee) James and her children, James Edwards James, and Mary Susan James, shortly after Jesse was assassinated. Zee is wearing a black dress and Mary Susan a black waistcloth to signify their mourning. (Photo courtesy of James R. Ross, grandson of Jesse Edwards James.)

Whippoorwill Creek. Their first child was born in Virginia and the rest, as follows, were born in Kentucky:

Mary James
Born: September 28, 1809
Died: July 23, 1877
Married: John Mimms, a cousin, 1827

William James
Born: September 11, 1811
Died: November 14, 1895
Married: Mary Ann Varble, December 2, 1843
Mary Ann Gibson Marsh, April 24, 1865

John R. James
Born: February 15, 1815
Died: October 25, 1887
Married: Amanda Polly Williams, September 1, 1836
Emily Bradley, 1872

Elizabeth James
Born: November 25, 1816
Died: November 2, 1904
Married: Tillman Howard West, 1837

Robert Sallee James
Born: July 17, 1818
Died: August 18, 1850, California
Married: Zerelda Cole, Kentucky, December 28, 1841˙

Nancy Gardner James
Born: September 13, 1821
Died: 1875
Married: George B. Hite, May 7, 1841

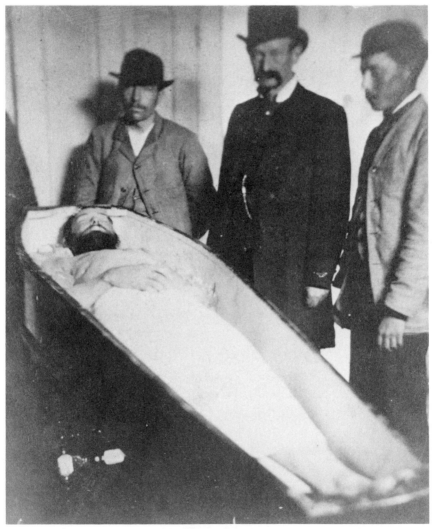

The body of Jesse Woodson James, packed in ice and displayed to the public after his assassination in St. Joseph, Missouri. St. Joseph City Marshal Enos Craig, center, stands guard with two deputies. (Photo courtesy Library of Congress collection.)

Thomas Martin James
  Born: April 8, 1823
  Died: December 25, 1903
  Married: Susan S. Woodward, Goochland
    County, Virginia
Drury Woodson James
  Born: November 14, 1826
  Died: July 1, 1910, California
  Married: Mary Louisa Dunn, September 15,
    1861

Mary James (who was to become mother-in-law to Jesse James) married John Mimms in 1827, and they had the following children: Robert, March 30, 1830; John Wilson, July 4, 1831; Drury Lilburn, May 9, 1833; David Woodson, August 23, 1835; Mary Elizabeth, October 18, 1837; Lucy Francis, July 14, 1829; George Tillman, November 6, 1841; Nancy Catherine, August 15, 1843; Zerelda Amanda, July 21, 1845; Thomas Martin, November 27, 1846; Sarah Ann, May 3, 1849; and Henry Clay, August 13, 1857. Their ninth child, Zerelda Amanda Mimms, married her first cousin, Jesse Woodson James, at her sister Lucy Browder's home in Kearney, Missouri on April 24, 1874. Zee, as she was called, died November 13, 1900.

William James was ordained a Methodist minister in 1832 and pastored his first church in Oldhorn County, Kentucky, where he was also a merchant. He married his first wife, Mary Ann Varble, on December 2, 1843. In 1847, he moved to Greenville, Missouri, where he was associated with his brother, Drury Woodson James, in a general store business. William married his second wife, Mary Ann Gibson Marsh, on April 24, 1865 near Platte City, Missouri. It was also Mary Ann's second marriage; her first husband was John S. Marsh.

William's second marriage failed, and Mary Ann moved to California to live with a son from her first marriage. William James had the following children: Julia, Thomas, William, Mary (Kirkpatrick), Laura (Dickson), George, Alice (Chapman), Luther, and Gustavus. William was the minister who performed the wedding for his nephew Jesse James and niece Zerelda Mimms. William tried to talk Zee out of marrying the outlaw Jesse, according to family history, but failed to do so. William is also referred to later as being instrumental in introducing Zerelda James, Jesse's mother, to her third husband, Dr. Reuben Samuel. William died in Kansas City, Missouri on November 14, 1895 and is buried in the Oak Grove Cemetery there.

John R. James's first marriage was to Amanda Polly Williams on September 1, 1836 in Logan County, Kentucky. Amanda was born June 28, 1817 in Logan County, Kentucky and died at Brownsville, Missouri on March 15, 1871. John then married Emily Bradley in 1872. John was a dentist and practiced in Arkansas and Missouri. John died in Carthage, Missouri on October 25, 1887. John and his first wife, Amanda, had the following children:

Robert Woodson James
    Born: July 1, 1838, Kentucky
    Died: March 26, 1922, Rich Hill, Missouri
    Married: Mary Elizabeth Deal, May 21, 1868

Susan Prudence James
    Born: November 25, 1845, Kentucky
    Died: February 9, 1919, Butler, Missouri
    Married: John Wesley Smith, December 27, 1866

John F. James
    Born: August 27, 1849

Died: 1925

Thomas M. James
    Born: August 16, 1852
    Died: February 27, 1854

Elizabeth James married Tillman Howard West[2] in 1837. According to records, the Wests lived in Jackson and Clay counties, Missouri, where Tillman was a successful businessman and was most influential in the early development of Kansas City, Missouri. He served on the Jackson County Railroad Committee and was a member of the Kansas City Board of Trade. Their children were as follows: Luther Virgil (died as an infant); Mary Mourning (died as an infant); Oscar Dunreath, 1840; Richard James, 1843; William Newton, 1847; Nancy Woodson; Amelia Putnam; Henry Clay. Nancy drowned at age fourteen and Amelia died at age ten.

Robert Sallee James[3] married Zerelda Cole in Kentucky on December 18, 1841 and moved to Missouri in 1842. The following children were born to them in Clay County: Alexander Franklin James, 1843; Robert R. James, 1845; Jesse Woodson James, 1847; and Susan Lavenia James (Parmer), 1849. Their son Robert lived only thirty-three days. A more detailed family history of the parents of Jesse and Frank James will be given later.

Nancy Gardner James married George B. Hite on June 7, 1841. They had the following children: Mary (Tulley), John, Olive, Irene, Robert Woodson,

2. See later for further information on the West and Howard families.

3. Robert Sallee James's middle name was given him in honor of a Baptist minister from Kentucky, Rev. Sallee, whom his parents admired.

The grave of Jesse James in Mt. Olivet Cemetery at Kearney, Missouri after it was moved from the James Farm, and Jesse's wife, Zerelda Mimms James.

Clarence Jeff, George, Cornelia, Lucy (Holloway), Jeff Davis, and Henry Clay. Olive, Irene, Cornelia, Jeff, and Henry all died as young children. Both Clarence Hite and his brother, Robert Woodson Hite, were known to be members of the James-Younger outlaw gang. Robert Hite was killed in 1881 by Robert Newton Ford, who was to later gain notoriety for killing Jesse James in 1882.

Thomas Martin James married Susan Woodward in Kansas City, Missouri. Thomas was a schoolteacher and later a successful businessman and civic leader in Kansas City, Missouri. They had two children, John Crawford James, 1848 and Luther Tillman James, 1850.

Drury Woodson James, youngest child of the John James family, was perhaps the most successful. He

The grave marker for Alexander Franklin (Frank) James and his wife, Annie Ralston James, Independence, Missouri. (Photos by author.)

married Louisa Dunn in 1861. Settling near San Luis Obispo in central California, he became a most successful cattle rancher and businessman. He is credited with helping to found the city of Paso Robles, California, which was originally a health resort. Drury also served in the California State Legislature and was mentioned as a possible candidate for governor. Robert James, Jesse and Frank James's father, visited his brother Drury a short time before he died in a California gold camp in 1850, a visit which will be elaborated on later. Evidence suggests that Robert and Drury were planning a gold mining venture. Drury Woodson James had the following children: Maria L. (Burns); William; Helen (Bennett); Lena; twins Caroline (1. Shackelford, 2. Maxwell) and Charles James; Edward James.

Zerelda James Samuel, mother of Jesse and Frank James, with her granddaughter Mary Susan James, Jesse's daughter. Photo taken on lawn of the James home.

ROBERT SALLEE JAMES

In *Background of a Bandit,* Joan Bemis and William Pullen point out that Robert James was, by any standard, the least likely of the John James children to sire two world-famous bandits. Born in Logan County, Kentucky on July 17, 1818, he was nine when his parents died. His sister Mary Mimms, herself only nineteen, then took Robert and her other small brothers and sisters into her home to raise with her own small children. Robert entered Georgetown

College in 1839 and graduated in 1843. While attending Georgetown College, Robert met Zerelda E. Cole, a student at a Georgetown convent, whom he married on December 28, 1841. Zerelda's father, James Cole, was killed in a horse accident when Zerelda was two years old. Her mother, Sallie Lindsay Cole, then married Robert Thomason in 1838 and moved to Missouri, leaving young Zerelda in Kentucky under the guardianship of Zerelda's uncle, James Lindsay. A few writers on James family history have suggested that Zerelda chose to stay in Kentucky since she did not get along with her stepfather, Robert Thomason.

After marriage, Robert took Zerelda to Missouri to visit the Thomasons in August of 1842. Robert then returned to Kentucky for postgraduate work at Georgetown College, leaving Zerelda, who was pregnant at the time, with the Thomasons. He planned on returning to Missouri by Christmas but could not because the Missouri River was frozen. In the spring of 1843, as river traffic was restored, Robert returned to Missouri. While Robert was away, his first son, Alexander Franklin James, was born on January 10, 1843.

The Reverend Robert James acquired a 275-acre farm near Kearney, Missouri in 1845. Georgetown College records indicate that Robert James continued to attend school there until 1847 and that he returned periodically for graduate work at that institution. Robert received a Master of Arts degree at Georgetown College in 1847.

Industrious Robert not only developed a large and successful farming operation in Clay County, Missouri, but also founded the New Hope, Mt. Pisgah, and Providence Baptist churches in the region. Robert James is also listed as one of the original organizers of

Jesse Edwards James, only son of Jesse James, left, with his uncle, John T. Samuel, right. (Photo courtesy of James R. Ross, grandson of Jesse Edwards James.)

Robert Franklin James, only son of Frank James, with his wife Mae. (Photo courtesy James R. Ross.)

the William Jewell College in Liberty, Missouri. These churches and William Jewell College are still operating today. Robert and Zerelda had the following children:

Alexander Franklin James
Born: January 10, 1843
Died: February 15, 1915
Married: Anna Ralston, June 1874

Robert R. James
Born: July 19, 1845
Died: August 21, 1845

Jesse Woodson James
  Born: September 5, 1847
  Died: April 3, 1882
  Married: Zerelda Amanda Mimms, April 24,
      1874
Susan Lavenia James
  Born: November 25, 1849
  Died: March 3, 1889
  Married: Allen H. Parmer, November 24, 1870

Robert James left his family in 1850 for the gold fields of California. Frank was seven, Jesse, three, and Susan, one at the time. His leaving a family on a frontier farm in such a manner has given cause for many previous writers to speculate that there must have been marriage problems. This theory is not sup-

Susan Lavenia James Parmer, only sister of Jesse and Frank James. (Photo courtesy of Carl W. Breihan.)

Allen H. Parmer, husband of Susan James, Jesse James's sister. Photo made at one of the last reunions of the Quantrill guerrilla forces. (Photo courtesy of the James Farm.)

ported, however, in the letters Robert wrote to his family while on the trip. Such letters expressed a deep love for Zerelda and his children and indicated a desire to return as soon as possible. It is, therefore, reasonable to assume that he was, as were thousands at the time, caught up in "gold fever." Hoping to strike it rich in the gold fields, he thought he would be better able to raise his family and expand his Baptist ministry. Whatever dreams Robert may have had, they were never to be realized, for soon after he arrived he became ill from food poisoning or some type of fever in a Placerville gold camp and died suddenly on August 18, 1850. He was buried in an unmarked grave.

ZERELDA ELIZABETH COLE

The lineage of Zerelda Cole James extends from John Cole, a native of Pennsylvania. He married a girl named Susanna. John died in Culpepper County, Virginia in 1757 and his wife in 1761. A son, Richard Cole, Sr., was born to John and Susanna in Pennsylvania in 1729. Richard Cole, Sr. settled lands near Midway, Kentucky. He married first Ann Hubbard in 1762 and second Emsey Margaret James on July 21, 1795 in Woodford County, Kentucky. Richard Cole owned a farm and tavern known as the Black Horse Tavern on the old Frankfort-Lexington Road. This tavern became a popular stopping place for travelers and politicians of the day. Henry Clay and John Jordan Crittenden, who served as Kentucky's governor for two years and later as a member of President Fillmore's cabinet, often visited and campaigned around Cole's popular tavern. This tavern has been recently restored.

As a result of the raw whiskey served and the often rowdy atmosphere of Cole's Tavern, the religious community of the region began referring to the tavern's location as Sodom. Richard Cole, Sr. died at Midway, Kentucky on November 21, 1814. Richard's children were as follows:

John Cole
   Married: Nancy Hines

Richard Cole, Jr.
   Born: April 23, 1763
   Died: July 9, 1839
   Married: Sally Yates

Jesse Cole
   Married: Nancy Sparks
           Elizabeth Roberts
           Elizabeth Hyatt

Rachael Cole
   Born: 1760
   Died: 1840
   Married: Willa Jett

Betsy Cole
   Married: Mr. Snape

Agnes Cole

Sallie Cole
   Married: Benjamin Graves

Alsey Alice Cole
   Born: June 20, 1769
   Died: July 7, 1813
   Married: Anthony Lindsay, Jr.

Lucy Cole
  Married: Jonathan Cropper

Richard Cole, Jr. married Sally Yates. He was a wealthy farmer and took over the operation of the family's Black Horse Tavern after his father died. Richard and Sally had the following children:

William Yates Cole
  Born: September 16, 1788
  Died: June 19, 1823

Mary (Polly) Cole
  Born: 1792
  Married: Elijah Finnie, July 18, 1806

Elizabeth Cole
  Married: Thomas Martin, April 23, 1814

Sally Cole
  Born: July 24, 1807
  Married: Henry B. Lewis

Jesse Cole
  Born: May 21, 1793
  Died: August 3, 1833

Amos Cole
  Born: February, 1798
  Died: Killed in a Cole Tavern fight, May 12, 1827

James Cole
  Born: September 8, 1804
  Died: February 27, 1827
  Married: Sallie Lindsay

James Cole married his first cousin, Sallie Lindsay, daughter of Anthony Lindsay and Alsey Cole. James and Sallie had the following children:

Zerelda E. Cole
  Born: January 29, 1825, Woodford County,
            Kentucky
  Died: February 10, 1911
  Married: Robert Sallee James, December 28,
            1841
          Benjamin Simms, September 30, 1852
          Dr. Reuben Samuel, September 25,
            1855

Jesse Richard Cole
  Born: November 29, 1826
  Died: November 16, 1895, Clay County,
            Missouri
  Married: Louisa G. Maret, December 26, 1846

James Cole died February 27, 1827 after falling from a horse. Zerelda was two years of age at the time of her father's death and her brother, Jesse Richard, only one. After her husband's death, Sallie and her two children resided with her father-in-law, Richard Cole, at the Black Horse Tavern until he died in 1839. After Richard's death, Sallie married Robert Thomason, a widower with six children, and the family, with the exception of Zerelda, moved to Clay County, Missouri.[4]

Zerelda despised Thomason, according to family history, and chose to stay in Kentucky. She resided with her uncle, James M. Lindsay, in Stamping Ground (Scott County, Kentucky) while attending school at the nearby Georgetown Catholic Convent.

After marrying Robert James on December 28, 1841, she moved with her husband to Clay County,

4. See later for details of the Thomason family.

Allen Pinkerton, founder of the Pinkerton Detective Agency, which the railroad companies employed to capture the James-Younger gang. (Photo courtesy of Smithsonian Institution Portrait Gallery, Washington, D.C.)

Missouri. While staying with her mother and step-father, the Thomasons, and while Robert finished seminary work at Georgetown College, her first child, Frank, was born in 1843. Robert returned, acquired a farm in 1845, and, after the birth of his son Jesse and daughter Susan, left for California, where he died in 1850.

Zerelda subsequently married a well-known Clay County farmer, Benjamin A. Simms, a widower with several children, on September 30, 1852. This was a very short and, by some accounts, unhappy union. Zerelda made the comment that Simms was a good husband and that their problems were over Zerelda's children. The James children apparently annoyed Simms and he wanted to send them away. These problems between Simms and Zerelda's children, and

Frank James at home at his ranch near Fletcher, Oklahoma between 1907 and 1913. Pictured are Frank James; Robert James, his son; and Annie James, his wife.

perhaps also Zerelda's somewhat domineering personality, resulted in a separation after only a few months of marriage. Simms conveniently died in a horse accident before they were divorced.

Certain previous James writers have indicated that the James boys were related to the Younger family who rode with Jesse and Frank James as the James-Younger gang. No family relationship between these families has ever been found. Recent research into the marriage of Zerelda James to Benjamin Simms, however, has uncovered a very insignificant relationship between the families through Simms's brief marriage to Zerelda James. Augusta Peters Inskeep, a niece of Simms's, married Thomas Coleman Younger, who was an uncle of Coleman, James, Robert, and John Younger, who were associated with the James-Younger gang. There was, therefore, this tenuous link between the families as a result of this marriage, but there was no blood relationship.

On September 25, 1855 Zerelda married once again, this time Dr. Reuben Samuel. This third marriage was by all accounts a happy union, and Dr. Samuel became the only father Frank, Jesse, and Susan James ever knew. (The Samuel family and the children of Zerelda and Reuben are covered later.)

Zerelda James Simms Samuel died from a heart ailment while on a train near Oklahoma City on February 10, 1911. She had been visiting her son Frank and his wife, Annie, near Fletcher, Oklahoma. Zerelda, at the age of eighty-six, was returning to her Clay County, Missouri farm home accompanied by Annie James at the time of her death. Zerelda was buried alongside her husband, Reuben Samuel, in the Mt. Olivet Cemetery in Kearney, Missouri.

ALEXANDER FRANKLIN JAMES

Frank James, the oldest child of the Reverend Robert James and Zerelda Cole James, was born at the home of Zerelda's parents in Clay County, Missouri on

January 10, 1843. After the outbreak of the Civil War, he joined the Confederate forces and participated in the Battle of Wilsons Creek. While Frank was hospitalized with measles in Springfield, Missouri, the hospital was taken by Union forces. Promising to switch his allegiance to the Union, he was released. Soon afterward, however, he joined the Confederate border guerrilla forces under the command of William Clarke Quantrill, where he was to serve until the war's end. Shortly after Quantrill was shot and left to die in Kentucky, Frank surrendered, in 1865, and returned to Missouri. Perhaps as a result of the extreme deprivation that faced ex-Confederate families along the Kansas-Missouri border country following the war, Frank and his brother Jesse teamed up with their former Quantrill guerrilla associates, the Younger brothers, to form the James-Younger gang, which would terrorize the nation for some seventeen years.

Frank married Anna Ralston on June 6, 1874. By this time he and his brother Jesse were highly sought-after outlaws. They eventually moved to the Nashville, Tennessee region, where Frank and Annie lived under the aliases of Ben J. and Fannie Woodson.

Frank and Annie only had one child:

Robert Franklin James
    Born: February 6, 1878
    Died: November 18, 1959, James Farm, Clay
            County, Missouri
    Married: May Sullivan
              Mae Sanboth

Tired of living as a wanted man and desiring to raise his son in peace, Frank James made arrangements through relatives and friends to surrender to Missouri Governor Thomas Crittenden on October 5, 1882. Frank faced trial on two occasions for murder and payroll robbery attributed to the James brothers. Since his brother Jesse had been assassinated before the trial occurred, the juries were unable to determine whether the crimes were committed by Frank, his brother Jesse, or by other parties. Also, by this time strong public sentiment supported Frank's release and eventually he was acquitted both times.

Having attained celebrity status by this time, Frank was in great demand at public events of all kinds. He also worked for a shoe company in Nevada, Missouri for a while, was in demand as a horse race starter, worked as a doorman at a St. Louis, Missouri theatre, and briefly greeted tourists at a Hot Springs, Arkansas theme park, Happy Hollow.

In 1909, while on a trip to visit his brother-in-law, Allen Parmer, in Wichita Falls, Texas, he acquired a ranch near Fletcher, Oklahoma, where he lived for about two years. Shortly after his mother died in 1911, Frank returned to the James family farm near Kearney, Missouri. There he spent the rest of his days greeting tourists and selling photographs and postcards. Frank died on the farm on February 15, 1915, and his body was cremated. His grave marker is alongside his wife Annie's in the Hill Park Cemetery in Independence, Missouri. Annie James remained on the farm until her death on July 6, 1944.

After Annie's death, Frank's only child, Robert, lived on the James farm and promoted the home of his famous father until his death. Robert's two marriages, first to May Sullivan and second to Mae Sanboth, were childless. He died on November 18, 1959 and was buried in Kearney.

JESSE WOODSON JAMES

Jesse, too young to be accepted in the army at the beginning of the Civil War, joined the guerrilla forces in mid-1864, and served under "Bloody Bill" Anderson. At fifteen years of age, legend says he was accepted only on Frank James's assurance that he would look after his young brother. Frank later served under Quantrill and Todd. As history shows, young Jesse James was soon to prove a leader and fearless soldier in spite of his youth. Participating in many battles and guerrilla skirmishes throughout the border region of Missouri, Kansas, and Arkansas, Jesse chose to go to Texas with a group of guerrilla associates in 1864 while his brother Frank rode to Kentucky with Quantrill. At the war's end, Jesse, along with several of his guerrilla associates, was riding into Missouri to surrender. As they approached the federal garrison under a white flag, the party was fired upon and Jesse was seriously wounded. This event, the extreme deprivation directed toward former Confederate guerrillas, and the post-war environment of Missouri no doubt greatly influenced the James brothers and many other Missouri ex-Confederates in becoming outlaws.

On April 24, 1874, Jesse married his first cousin, Zerelda (Zee) Amanda Mimms, at the home of Zee's sister, Lucy Mimms Browder, in Kearney, Missouri. Because Jesse was already a highly sought-after outlaw, the Reverend William James, brother of Jesse's father, tried to discourage the union, but he failed to do so and finally performed the ceremony. A "wanted man," Jesse took Zee to Nashville, Tennessee around 1875, where he hoped they could live in peace under his alias of John Davis Howard. In Nashville the following children were born to Jesse and Zee:

Jesse Edwards James
Born: August 31, 1875, Nashville, Tennessee
Died: March 26, 1951, California
Married: Stella McGowan, January 24, 1900

Twins: Gould and Montgomery James
Died as infants

Mary Susan James
Born: June 17, 1879, Nashville, Tennesee
Died: October 11, 1935, Kansas City, Missouri
Married: Henry Lafayette Barr, March 6, 1901

Jesse Edwards James was named for John N. Edwards, a Kansas City newspaper editor admired by Jesse James for the sympathetic treatment his editorials always gave the outlaw. Bill Ryan, an outlaw associate of Jesse and Frank James, was arrested in a saloon near Nashville on March 25, 1881. Fearing Ryan's arrest might result in their being discovered, Jesse and Frank, along with their families, left Nashville. Jesse took his family to Kansas City, and later to St. Joseph, Missouri, where he rented a home under the alias of Thomas Howard.

Charles Ford, brother of the infamous assassin Robert Ford, moved in with Jesse while Charles was hiding from the law. Treachery began when Charles convinced Jesse to let his brother Robert participate in a planned bank robbery. Bob Ford had previously conceived a plan to capture Jesse for the reward offered for his apprehension. Bob and Charlie, guests in Jesse's home, carefully waited for the right opportunity. After breakfast on April 3, 1882, Jesse, Bob, and

Charles left the kitchen and went into the parlor. Jesse removed his gun belt and laid it on a day bed. Noticing a picture was crooked or, as some accounts observe, needed dusting, Jesse stepped on a chair to attend to the problem. At that moment Bob Ford shot Jesse behind the right ear. Jesse James was originally buried in the lawn of the Jameses' farm home. Several years later his body was exhumed and removed to the Mt. Olivet Cemetery in Kearney, Missouri.

Bob and Charlie Ford were immediately ostracized by the American public for the cowardly way they brought Jesse James to his death. Charlie Ford succumbed to the ridicule and committed suicide. Bob Ford, apparently with the reward money he received for his treachery, journeyed to Creede, Colorado, where he opened a saloon. Ed O'Kelley had several arguments with Ford over money, women, or perhaps the way Ford killed Jesse. O'Kelley killed Robert Ford on June 8, 1892 in Ford's saloon.

Zerelda (Zee) James died at her sister's home in Kansas City, Missouri on November 13, 1900 and is buried next to Jesse in the Mt. Olivet Cemetery in Kearney, Missouri.

SUSAN LAVENIA JAMES (PARMER)

Susan Lavenia, the only daughter of Robert and Zerelda James, born on November 25, 1849, was only a few months old when her father died in California. The only father she ever really knew, as will be described later, was her mother's third husband, Dr. Reuben Samuel.

There is no record indicating an early association between the James family and the Parmer family of Liberty, in Clay County, Missouri, although Liberty was only a few miles from the James farm. The son of Isaac and Barbara Parmer, Allen Parmer,[5] who was to become the husband of Susan James, was born on May 6, 1848. He was, therefore, nine months younger than Jesse James. Allen is referred to in many creditable books on Quantrill as being among the leaders of Quantrill's guerrilla organization. With Frank James, he participated in the infamous Lawrence, Kansas raid, under Quantrill's command, and in other major guerrilla skirmishes throughout the border country. Parmer was listed as one of the Quantrill party, again with Frank James, that surrendered at the war's end on September 26, 1865 at Samuels Station, Kentucky. Since Parmer was apparently closely associated with Jesse and Frank James as a member of the guerrilla forces, it is reasonable to assume that he first met Susan James through her brothers.

Other writers have also indicated that Parmer, with other former Quantrill associates, joined the James brothers in outlaw activities following the war. The

5. Question has been raised by past writers over the correct spelling of Allen Parmer's name. Although census records in Missouri, Arkansas, and Texas, as well as Civil War records, spell his family name Palmer, this writer believes his true name was Parmer, since it appears on all of the family's grave markers so spelled. Early record takers could quite easily have misspelled the Parmer name since the name Palmer was more predominant.

The home of Jesse and Frank James's aunt and uncle, Nancy and George Hite, near Adairville, Kentucky as it appears today. The James brothers often took refuge from the law here. (Photo courtesy of Ted Yeatman.)

only documentation of Parmer's involvement with the James gang after the war, however, was his arrest years later in Texas. Missouri authorities arrested him in Texas and returned him to Kansas City, where he was to be tried for the Glendale train robbery which occurred on October 8, 1879. However, witnesses could not positively identify him and he was soon released.

When he learned of his sister's impending marriage to Allen Parmer and apparently strongly opposing the marriage, Jesse James reportedly attempted suicide by taking sixteen grains of morphine. Jesse was suffering badly at the time from old war wounds and hiding out at his uncle George Hite's home near Adairville, Kentucky. Jesse may have been concerned about the marriage, but most past writers prefer to believe that the overdose of morphine was motivated by his pain and not despair over his sister's decision. Revived by a Dr. D. J. Simmons, Jesse was later embarrassed over the incident.

Allen and Susan were married in Clay County on November 24, 1870. They then moved to Boonsboro (now Cane Hill), Arkansas to be near Allen's parents, who had acquired land there in January of that year. The log home Allen built in Arkansas still stands. Susan taught school in the Bethesda community near her home. Their first child, Robert Archie Parmer, was born in Arkansas in 1872. The Parmers left Arkansas in early 1874 and settled near Sherman, Texas, where Susan once more taught school and Allen took employment in railroad construction and as a cattle drover.

When Jesse James and his wife, Zee, were married on April 4, 1874, they reportedly honeymooned for several weeks at his sister's home in Sherman. Parmer was a loyal Confederate and, like the James brothers, no doubt had a secret desire for the South to rise again. He may have supported Jesse and Frank's outlaw activities after the war, but his actual participation in the gang is doubtful. Susan, a leader in the Baptist church and a very religious, highly respected lady wherever she went, would not have approved of her husband becoming involved in outlaw activities.

Sometime around 1882 the Parmers moved to Wichita Falls, Texas and later to nearby Archer City, Texas, where Allen became foreman of the J. Stone Land and Cattle Co.

The Parmers had the following children:

Robert Archie Parmer
    Born: 1872, Arkansas
    Died: July 9, 1883

Flora Parmer
  Born: June 13, 1877
  Died: 1926
  Married: William Benson

Zelma Parmer
  Born: December 19, 1879
  Died: February 6, 1972
  Married: George R. Edwards

Allen Parmer, Jr.
  Born: 1882
  Died: 1885

Susan Kate Parmer
  Born: December 25, 1885
  Died: October 6, 1903
  Never married

Feta Parmer
  Born: September 14, 1887
  Died: August 20, 1978
  Married: Bert A. Rose

A stillborn son
  Born: March 2, 1889

Susan James Parmer died at age thirty-nine on March 3, 1889 from childbirth complications. She was buried alongside the three children who had preceded her in death in Riverside Cemetery in Wichita Falls.

After Susan's death, Allen Parmer married a former housekeeper, Sarah Katherine "Aunt Kitty" Ogden, from Lexington, Missouri. After giving up ranching in 1905, Allen again worked at railroad construction for several years before retiring to Alpine, Texas in 1920. Allen died suddenly on October 20, 1927 while visiting in the Wichita Falls home of an old friend and former

Quantrill associate, Claude Miller. His second wife, Kitty, died on December 31, 1944 in an Austin, Texas Confederate home.

Dorothy Rose, daughter of Feta Parmer Rose, married Robert M. Higbie. Dorothy died July 15, 1987 near Gainesville, Texas. Several descendants of Zelma Parmer Edwards have also visited the James farm in Missouri.

JESSE EDWARDS JAMES

Except for twin sons who died at birth, Jesse Edwards James was the only son of Jesse and Zee James. He was born in Nashville, Tennessee on August 31, 1875 while Jesse and Zee were living under the alias of Howard.

Jesse named his son in honor of John Newman Edwards, perhaps the best friend the James brothers had, who has often been credited with creating the legend of Jesse James. As a newspaper reporter for the Lexington, Missouri *Expositor,* and the St. Louis *Republican,* and eventually (in 1868) as founder of the Kansas City *Times,* Edwards, a Southern sympathizer, treated the James brothers kindly in his many editorials about the gang's activities. During the Civil War, Edwards served under Gen. Jo Shelby in what became known as the Iron Brigade. With other Southerners, Edwards supported the James-Younger gang's outlaw activities, which he felt were somewhat justified. The romance he injected into his editorials helped to create the folk hero status of the James brothers.

Jesse Edwards was raised by his mother in Kansas City after his father's assassination. He attended law school and practiced there. He later moved to Los Angeles, California. He married Stella McGowan on January 24, 1900 in Kansas City, Missouri, and they had the following children:

Lucille Martha James
  Born: December 21, 1900
  Died: June 17, 1988
  Married: Frank Lewis, September 1, 1931

Josephine Francis James
  Born: April 20, 1902
  Died: March 31, 1964
  Married: Ronald Ross, September 2, 1925

Jessie Estelle James
  Born: August 27, 1906
  Died: February 2, 1987
  Married: Mervyn Baumel, May 23, 1931

Ethel Rose James
  Born: July 10, 1908
  Married: Calvin T. Owens, October 16, 1937

Lucille and Frank Lewis had the following children in California:

James Curtis Lewis
  Born: November 28, 1935
  Married: Angelica Gloria Alvarado, April 12, 1958
  Children: Christopher James Lewis
        Born: January 15, 1959
        Jennifer Angelica Lewis
        Born: July 23, 1965

Josephine Francis and Ronald Ross had the following children:

James Randal Ross
   Born: July 6, 1926
   Married: Rosemary Henderson, September 2,
      1950
   Children: Bonnie Jo Ross
      Born: April 30, 1957
      Married: James Edward Barnes, July
         14, 1982
      Randal Glenn Ross
      Born: August 9, 1961
      David James Ross
      Born: July 27, 1963
      Elizabeth Danielle Ross
      Born: November 29, 1968

   Jessie Estelle and Mervyn Baumel had the following children in California:

Donald James Baumel
   Born: March 24, 1933
Diane June Baumel
   Born: March 24, 1933
   Married: James Fairchild, October 11, 1953
   Children: Michael James Fairchild
      Born: March 7, 1960

   Ethel Rose and Calvin Owens have no children.
   James R. Ross, son of Josephine and Ronald Ross and grandson of Jesse Edwards James, presently serves as the superior court judge in Orange County, California.

MARY SUSAN JAMES

Mary Susan, Jesse and Zee James's only daughter, was named after Jesse's sister, Susan, and Zee's mother, Mary. Born in Nashville, Tennessee on June 17, 1879, she was only three when her father was assassinated by Bob Ford. She was raised by her mother in Kansas City and married Henry Lafayette Barr on March 6, 1901. Mary Susan and Henry Barr had the following children:

Lawrence H. Barr
   Born: October 16, 1902
   Died: February 25, 1984
   Married: Thelma Duncan (Born: January 21,
         1906)
   Children: Elizabeth Ann Barr
         Born: October 11, 1937

Forster Ray Barr
   Born: October 11, 1904
   Died: June 23, 1977
   Married: Gertie Essary (Born: May 11, 1914)

Chester A. Barr
   Born: May 27, 1907
   Died: March 22, 1984
   Married: Beatrice Holloway (divorced)
   Children: Frederick Arthur Barr
        Born: September 8, 1937

Henrietta Barr
   Born: March 14, 1913
   Died: October 10, 1913

Thelma Duncan Barr and Lawrence Barr at the 1983 James family reunion. George Warfel's painting of Jesse James, Lawrence Barr's grandfather, is at right. (Photo by author.)

Lawrence Barr attended his last James family reunion on the James Farm in 1983. This writer had occasion to meet Mr. Barr at that reunion and to discuss this James family project with him. He admitted that until his later years he had always been somewhat ashamed of being the grandson of the outlaw Jesse James and kept what family history he knew to himself. He realized late in life, however, that the folk hero status of Jesse James made preserving the James family history important, and before his death in 1984 he contributed greatly to the family history recorded here. Since his death, his wife, Thelma Barr, has continued to serve as an honorary member of the Friends of the James Farm Board of Directors and has greatly assisted in the preparation of this history.

Fielding and Mary White Samuel, parents of Dr. Reuben Samuel.

Fielding Samuel, father of Dr. Reuben Samuel, with members of the Samuel family at their Clifty, Arkansas home.

CHAPTER 2

The
Samuel
Family

REUBEN SAMUEL
(THE FIRST)

Reuben Samuel of Virginia was the father of Reuben Samuel, Jr., who was born in Goochland County, Virginia on January 7, 1761. Reuben Jr. married Mary (Polly) Letcher, who was born, also in Goochland County, Virginia, on April 25, 1770. Mary Letcher was the sister of a Kentucky governor. Reuben Samuel, Jr. died in Frankfort, Kentucky on January 1, 1832. His wife, Mary, also died there on March 30, 1836. The one known son of Reuben, Jr. and Mary was:

Fielding Samuel
    Born: May 26, 1803, Kentucky
    Died: May 4, 1886, Clifty, Arkansas
    Married: Louisa Bond, Kentucky
         Mary White, December 25, 1838

Fielding's first wife, Louisa Bond, died in Kentucky prior to 1838, and he then married Mary White in Kentucky. Fielding and his first wife, Louisa, had the following known children:

H. B. Samuel
    Born: 1827, Kentucky

Reuben Samuel
    Born: January 12, 1828, Owen County, Kentucky
    Died: March 1, 1908, St. Joseph, Missouri
    Married: Zerelda Cole James Simms, September 12, 1855

Fielding and his second wife, Mary White, had the following children:

Prudence Samuel
    Born: 1841, Kentucky
    Died: 1907, Tecumseh, Oklahoma
    Married: Richard Burden

William P. Samuel
    Born: 1843, Kentucky

Fielding Samuel, Jr.
    Born: January 27, 1845, Kentucky
    Died: July 5, 1937, Clifty, Arkansas
    Married: Cornelius Liggon

Addelaide Samuel[1]
    Born: 1846, Kentucky
    Died: Tecumseh, Oklahoma
    Married: Not known

M. E. Samuel (female)
    Born: 1848, Kentucky
    Apparently died as child

1. Little is known of Addelaide Samuel. Referred to by the family as Aunt Addie, she is believed to be the fourth child of Fielding and Mary White Samuel and lived in the Tecumseh, Oklahoma region.

Edward Madison Samuel
Born: September 12, 1851, Clay County,
Missouri
Died: July 11, 1935, Clifty, Arkansas
Married: Nancy Cherubia Vaughn

Since Fielding and Mary White Samuel's youngest
child, Edward, was born in Missouri in 1851 and since
the family appears on the 1850 Missouri census, the
family apparently moved from Kentucky to Missouri
between 1848 and 1850. The Samuel farm was only
about one mile from the James farm which Robert and
Zerelda James had acquired in Clay County in 1845.
The James and Samuel families were, therefore, early
Clay County neighbors, and it is likely that they were
acquainted.

Tired of constant questions and accusations by law
officials that he was protecting his outlaw relatives the
James boys, Fielding Samuel left Missouri with his
family sometime around 1875 and settled lands near
the Clifty community in northwest Arkansas. The log
home they built there still stands, and it remains in the
Samuel family. Fielding died in Arkansas on May 4,
1886 and is buried in the Clifty, Arkansas cemetery.

Nothing is known of Fielding's first child, H. B.
Samuel, who was born in Kentucky in 1827 except that
she was listed on the 1850 Missouri census but not on
the 1860 census.

DR. REUBEN SAMUEL

Reuben Samuel returned to Kentucky for a while
after helping his father, stepmother, sister Addelaide,

Dr. Reuben Samuel, stepfather of Frank, Jesse, and Susan James.

half-sister Prudence, and half-brother Fielding, Jr. move to Missouri. From 1850 to 1851, Reuben attended the Ohio Medical College in Cincinnati, Ohio. Returning to Missouri in 1852, he practiced medicine for two years in Liberty, Missouri. In 1854, he moved his practice to the Greenville community and set up offices in a general store owned and operated by William James, who was a brother of Robert James, the father of Jesse and Frank James.

It is not known if Reuben knew Zerelda James prior to this time. Since the Samuel farm was only about one mile from the James farm it is reasonable to assume they probably had at least a slight acquaintance. Indi-

Sarah (Sallie) Louis Samuel Nickolson, half-sister to Frank, Jesse, and Susan James.

cations are, however, that their first real familiarity came about through William James, who was Zerelda James's brother-in-law. Zerelda had lost her first husband, Robert James, in 1850, and her second husband, Benjamin Simms, had been killed. Reuben fell in love with Zerelda, who was described as "very good looking and lively," and they were married in September of 1855. Zerelda's children, Frank James, Jesse James, and Susan James were ages twelve, eight, and six respectively, at the time of their mother's third and last marriage.

Living with Zerelda's children on the James farm, Dr. Reuben Samuel and Zerelda had the following children of their own:

Sarah (Sallie) Louisa Samuel
   Born: December 26, 1858
   Died: September 15, 1915
   Married: William Nicholson, November 28,
         1878

Children: James (Archie)
Born: October 19, 1879
Died: January 28, 1961
Married: Belle

Franklin
Born: March 31, 1882
Died: 1947
Married: Effie Robertson

Fred Brocton
Born: October 9, 1891
Died: 1969
Married: Eula Holt

John Thomas Samuel
Born: December 25, 1861
Died: March 15, 1932
Married: Norma L. Maret, July 22, 1885

Fannie Quantrill Samuel
Born: October 18, 1863
Died: May 30, 1922
Married: Joe C. Hall, December 30, 1880
Children: Jesse Franklin
Born: October 8, 1881
Died: August 29, 1955
Married: Allene Marguerite Groom

Susan
Born: March 12, 1887
Died: November 18, 1948
Married: Lawson Race

George
Born: August 3, 1890
Died: March 3, 1963
Married: Emma Jean Riley
Addie Mae Webber
Ruth Tepp

Archie Peyton Samuel
  Born: July 26, 1866
  Died: January 26, 1875

Perry Samuel[2]
  Born: 1862
  Died: March 1, 1936
  Children: Dora
        Married: Robert Iowa
        Ruth
        Married: Matt Davidson

In May of 1863, a regiment of Federal militia rode up to the Samuel farm seeking information as to the whereabouts of Zerelda's son Frank and the Confederate guerrilla camps. By this time, Frank James had become a member of Quantrill's border guerrilla forces, and the Union soldiers hoped to force the Samuels to give them information that might be of help in locating the guerrilla camps. Taking Reuben behind the Samuels' home, the Federal troops put a rope around his neck and threw it over the limb of a large tree. The soldiers then threatened to hang Reuben if he didn't give the desired information. Reuben refused and was hanged for a few minutes, then released. Repeatedly, the soldiers hanged and revived Reuben, who stalwartly kept his silence until the Union soldiers gave up, leaving Reuben hanging. The soldiers then found young Jesse James plowing in the fields, surrounded him, and demanded information about his brother Frank from him. Still receiving

2. Perry Samuel was the half-black son of one of Reuben Samuel's slaves. Some writers have indicated that John T. Samuel was his father. Since John T. was very young at the time, it is more reasonable to credit Reuben with being the boy's father.

no information, the soldiers severely whipped Jesse and rode away leaving him lying bloody and battered in the field. Half crawling back to the farmhouse, he found his mother desperately trying to revive her husband, while Jesse's sister Susan, half-sister Sarah, and small half-brother John T. looked on.

The tragic events of that day created such hatred in young Jesse James, not yet sixteen years of age, that he left home to find his brother Frank and to join Quantrill's Confederate guerrilla forces. It was unquestionably these events that motivated Jesse James to become a leader within these Confederate forces in spite of his youth.

Reuben Samuel did not die from his hanging by Federal troops, but his brain was deprived of oxygen for so long during the episode that his mind was affected. Dr. Samuel was never to recover mentally from the hanging and could no longer practice medicine regularly. He was the only father the James children ever really knew, and by virtue of the love and kindness shown to them all and because of the courage and loyalty shown by his willingness to give his own life rather than betray his stepson, Dr. Samuel was revered by the James boys.

To escape the ravages of war throughout the border country around their Missouri farm, Zerelda took her ailing husband and children to Rulo, Nebraska. Although they returned and rebuilt their farm after the war, Reuben eventually had to be admitted to a home for the mentally insane in St. Joseph, Missouri. He died there on March 1, 1908, and his body was returned to Kearney, Missouri, where he is buried in the Mt. Olivet Cemetery.

Reuben and Zerelda's youngest son, Archie Peyton Samuel, was killed by an explosive which was thrown into the James home by railroad detectives, thought to be the Pinkertons, on January 26, 1875. Hoping to find Jesse and Frank James, the lawmen threw some type of metal flare through the window to light up the home. Zerelda hurriedly shoved the burning mass into the fireplace, causing the object to explode. The explosion killed Archie, who was only eight years of age, and mangled Zerelda's right arm below the elbow so badly that it had to be amputated. The lawmen and the Pinkerton agency were highly criticized for their action, and this event was instrumental in the creation of favorable public sentiment toward the James brothers.

PRUDENCE SAMUEL

Prudence Samuel, born in Kentucky, came to Missouri with her parents, Fielding and Mary White Samuel, her brother Fielding, Jr., half-brother Reuben, and half-sister Addelaide, in 1847. She married Richard Burden in Clay County, Missouri and had at least one child there, Richard Henry Lee Burden, in 1864. The fact that her half-brother, Reuben, was Jesse and Frank James's stepfather made her their aunt by marriage. Prudence was very proud of this relationship to the notorious James brothers and often told her family about it. She attended Jesse James's funeral in 1882.

It is believed that Prudence went to Arkansas with the other members of the Samuel family for a while before she and her husband left for Indian Territory (now Oklahoma), where they settled near the Tecumseh community. Her son, Richard Henry Lee Burden, often said that he was spending the night with his cousin, Archie Peyton Samuel, at the James home on the night the Pinkerton bomb was thrown into the home, exploded, and killed Archie, but this story cannot be verified. The children of Prudence and Richard are as follows:

Richard Henry Lee Burden
Born: 1864
Died: 1917
Married: Arie Calico
Children: Alva Lester Burden

Will Burden

Anna Burden
Married: Sam Cobb

WILLIAM P. SAMUEL

Born in Kentucky in 1843, William P. is listed through the 1860 census as living with his parents in Clay County, Missouri. Nothing else is known of this child at this time. Descendants of William P. Samuel's brother, Edward Samuel, believe his middle name was Patterson, since the name William Patterson was also given to later generations.

FIELDING SAMUEL, JR.

Fielding Samuel, Jr. was the son of Fielding and his second wife, Mary White Samuel. He moved from Missouri to Arkansas with his father and mother, brother Edward, sister Prudence, and half-sister Addelaide around 1875. He married Cornelius Liggon. Cornelius died at their Clifty, Arkansas home on December 16, 1923, and Fielding, Jr. died there on July 5, 1937. Fielding and Cornelius had the following children:

Mary Samuel
   Born: September 28, 1868
   Died: May 13, 1929

Will Samuel
   Married: Cora Corville
   Children: Happie (Davidson)
               Bertie (Van Hoosen)
               Carney (Pogue)
               Lema (Teeters)
               Valley
               Raymond (adopted)

Fannie Samuel
   Married: Will Capps
   Children: Sam
               Henry
               Larse
               Blanche

Otho V. Samuel
  Born: November 23, 1891
  Died: August 31, 1971
  Married: Rena Pittendrigh
  Children: Nina Velma (Walker)
             Everette Fielding
             James Cornelius
             Francis Orlena (Carrier)
             Joe L.

ADDELAIDE SAMUEL

Addelaide is believed to have been the fourth child of Fielding and his second wife, Mary White, and was a half-sister to Rueben Samuel; little is known of her at this time. Family letters of Alva Lester Burden, grandson of Prudence Samuel Burden, refer to her as Aunt Addie living in Indian Territory near the community of Tecumseh, Oklahoma. Nothing more is known of a possible marriage, children, or place of death at this time.

EDWARD MADISON SAMUEL

Edward M. Samuel, son of Fielding and his second wife, Mary White Samuel, was born in Clay County,

The Edward Madison Samuel family. Front row; Charles, Edward, William, Nancy Cherubia Vaughn Samuel, and Robert. Back row; Neva Samuel (Archer), Mag Samuel (Stillwell), Walter, and Julia Samuel (Luck).

Missouri on September 12, 1851. He married Nancy Cherubia Vaughn, the daughter of George Washington Vaughn, in Madison County, Arkansas on August 29, 1880. Nancy Cherubia was born in Arkansas in 1860 and died there in 1930. Edward left Clay County, Missouri with his family shortly after he was arrested and accused of being a picket for and protecting his half-nephews, Jesse and Frank James, in 1875.

Railroad detectives, believed to have been working for the Pinkerton Agency, surrounded the James cabin on the night of January 26, 1875. Thinking the James brothers were inside, they threw a flare through the cabin window to light up the room. Zerelda James Samuel kicked the flare into the fireplace, causing the object to explode. The explosion killed her son, Archie

The Samuel family home near Clifty, Arkansas as it appears today. The home still remains in the Samuel family. (Photo by author.)

Peyton Samuel, age eight, who was sleeping in the room and also mangled Zerelda's arm so badly it had to be amputated at the elbow. Apparently Ed Samuel was arrested the next morning. The incident was reported in the Kansas City *Times* as follows on January 29, 1875: "A posse of 46 men, formed by Clay County Sheriff John S. Groom, captured three men accused of being pickets for the James brothers. These men were Ed T. Miller (brother of Clell Miller, known to ride with the James gang), George James (a cousin of the James boys), and Ed Samuel." They were taken to the Liberty jail where they were interviewed by the Kansas City *Times.* Among other things Ed Samuel reportedly said, "I am past 22 years old, I ain't married but if I get out of this I am going to be. I heard the fight at Mrs. Samuel's and next morning went over to work on the sick. When I get out of this I'm going to get the hell out of Missouri." Constant harassment by law officials apparently caused these relatives of Jesse and Frank James to leave Missouri and relocate in Arkansas.

Ed Samuel often related stories of Jesse and Frank James visiting their Uncle Ed at his Clifty, Arkansas farm. When in the region, the James brothers sometimes used the alias of Vaughn and claimed to be brothers of Ed Samuel's wife, Nancy Cherubia Vaughn Samuel, to prevent suspicion.

Ed Samuel died at his Clifty, Arkansas home on July 11, 1935. His wife, Nancy Cherubia, preceded him in death in 1930. Both are buried in the Clifty, Arkansas cemetery. Ed and Nancy had the following children:

Geneva Samuel
    Born: July 18, 1881
    Died: May 20, 1963
    Married: Ralph Archer
    Children: Loren
              Mamie (Moore)
              Harvey
              Jewell (Stafford)
              Paul
              Floyd
              Nina

Margaret Samuel
    Born: February 26, 1883
    Died: December 18, 1965
    Married: Robert Stillwell
    Children: Arch
              Don
              Nancy (Milt Die)

Walter Samuel
    Married: Cassie Chestnut
    Children: Jane
              Billie

Julie C. Samuel
 Born: February 24, 1887
 Died: May 29, 1913
 Married: William Luck

Charles M. Samuel
 Born: March 18, 1889
 Died: May 29, 1974
 Married: Ada Rogers
 Children: Clifford C.
                    Lawrence Elmo

Robert Samuel
 Born: September 22, 1892
 Died: February 24, 1918

William Patterson Samuel
 Born: 1894
 Died: 1978
 Married: Sarah (Bessie) Sandlain
 Children: Keith Samuel
                    Kenneth Samuel

Maisie Samuel
 Born: January 13, 1900
 Married: Harry Mobley
 Children: Nancy Cara (died young)

Maisie Samuel Mobley of Prairie Grove, Arkansas is the oldest surviving child of the Edward Madison Samuel family. Her only daughter, Nancy Cara, died as a child. Maisie is eighty-six years of age at the time of this writing and contributed greatly in recording the Samuel family history. A great many descendants of the Samuel family still live throughout northwest Arkansas, and they keep alive their many family stories about their famous relatives.

CHAPTER 3

The Woodson—Poor—Mimms Families

Studying James family history, one finds the Poor, Woodson, and Mimms families all closely interrelated and often mentioned. There are many instances of marriage between these families, and several marriages appear between first and second cousins. The Woodson name appears often as a middle name. Jesse Woodson James received his middle name from his great-grandmother, Elizabeth Woodson, who married his great-grandfather, Robert Poor, in the 1700s. Robert and Elizabeth's daughter, Mary (Polly) Poor, married John M. James in 1807. John M. James's brother Richard also married a Poor, Mary G. Poor, who is believed to have been a sister of Polly Poor.

Frank James chose to use his great-grandmother's maiden name, Woodson, as an alias. During his years in Nashville, Tennessee, Frank James used the name Ben J. Woodson.

The lineage and close connections of these families can be outlined as follows:

Shadrack Mimms
  Born: 1734
  Died: 1777
  Married: (1) Mary Allen, February 3, 1754
         (2) Elizabeth Woodson

Child: Elizabeth Mimms

Elizabeth Mimms
  Born: April 3, 1769
  Died: 1823
  Married: Robert Poor, February 7, 1789
  Child: Mary (Polly) Poor

Mary (Polly) Poor
  Born: 1790
  Died: 1827
  Married: John M. James, Virginia, March 26,
          1807
  Children: Mary (married John Mimms)
            William (married Varble and Marsh)
            John (married Amanda Williams and
                Emily Bradley)
            Elizabeth (married Tillman Howard
                West)
            Robert Sallee (married Zerelda Cole)
            Nancy Gardner (married George Hite)
            Thomas Martin (married Susan
                Woodward)
            Drury Woodson (married Louisa
                Dunn)

Jesse James married his first cousin, Zerelda
Amanda Mimms, on April 24, 1874, Zerelda being the
daughter of John Mimms and Mary James, who was
Jesse's father's sister. John James and Polly Poor James
were, therefore, the grandparents of both Jesse James
and his wife, Zerelda.

CHAPTER 4

The
Thomason
Family

Zerelda Cole and her brother, Jesse Richard Cole,
were the children of James Cole and Sallie (Lindsay)
Cole. James was killed by a horse in an accident on
February 27, 1827. Sallie then took her children to live
with James Cole's father, Richard Cole, Jr., at his
family's Black Horse Tavern at Midway, Kentucky.
Sallie remained there with her children until 1838. Her
father-in-law, Richard Cole, Jr., died in 1839. Sallie
married Robert Thomason, who was a widower with
six children, in 1838. Robert and Sallie, along with
Sallie's son, Jesse Richard Cole, then moved to Clay
County, Missouri. Zerelda chose to stay in Kentucky
under the guardianship of her uncle, James M.
Lindsay. Zerelda attended school at a convent in
Georgetown, where she met Robert Sallee James, who
was attending Georgetown College.

Robert and Sallie Thomason had the following
children in Clay County, Missouri:

Elizabeth Thomason
    Married: Thomas Patton

Martha Ann Thomason
    Married: Robert Mimms, September 8, 1870

Mary Alice Thomason
    Born: December 2, 1844

Married: Marrett Jones Scott, July 13, 1876
Children: One known son

Robert James and his wife, Zerelda, went to Clay County, Missouri in 1842, before Robert's graduation from college. Leaving Zerelda with her mother and stepfather, the Thomasons, Robert James returned to Kentucky for graduate work at Georgetown College. Zerelda's first child, Alexander Franklin James, was born on January 10, 1843 at the Thomasons' home.

According to a Thomason researcher, Russ Thomason of Morehead, Kentucky, John S. Thomason, who was a Clay County sheriff, is often mentioned in books about Jesse and Frank James as a lawman who constantly tracked and tried to capture the James brothers. This sheriff, John Thomason, was a nephew of Robert Thomason, who had married the James brothers' grandmother.

CHAPTER 5

The
West and Howard
Families

As was outlined earlier, Elizabeth James was a sister of Jesse, Frank, and Susan James's father, Robert Sallee James. Elizabeth married Tillman Howard West. Since the James and West families were apparently closely associated, and since it was through this family connection that Jesse James got the Howard alias he often used, what is currently known of this West family is outlined here as follows:

William West
    Born: 1752, Chatham County, North Carolina
    Died: 1842, Simpson County, Kentucky
    Married: Angeline Clendennen or Clendenning
    Known children: Isabelle West
                Married: Hiram Holcolm,
                1813
             John West
             Born: February 19, 1794
             Died: April 30, 1859,
                Crawford County,
                Arkansas
             Married: Lavenia Jane
                Howard, January 7, 1814
             Leonard West

James West
Born: August 27, 1772,
   Simpson County,
   Kentucky
Died: 1844, Kentucky
Married: Mary Mourning
   Howard, October 1, 1807
Mary Anne (Polly) West
Married: Milliken
Elsie West
Married: James Milliken

James West
   Born: August 27, 1772, Simpson County,
      Kentucky
   Died: 1844, Simpson County, Kentucky
   Married: Mary Mourning Howard
   Children: Preston Milton West
      Born: August 28, 1808, Kentucky
      Died: June 19, 1888
      Married: Martha A. Hail
      Children: Angeline Clendennen
         Howard West (1830–1904)
         James Durham West (1838–
            1921)
         Olivia Cordelia West (born
            1840)
         Edgar Alexander West
            (1843–1914)
         Martha Adelia West (born
            1846)
   Tillman Howard West
      Born: May 8, 1810, Simpson County, Kentucky
      Died: October 3, 1884, Kansas City, Missouri
      Married: Elizabeth James

This rare photo of Jesse James, left, and Frank James was confirmed as genuine by noted James photo expert George Warfel. (Courtesy of Joe Ann Byland of Carrollton, IL and Sandra Reynolds Ogg of Brighton, IL.)

Children: Luther Virgil West (died young)
Mary Mourning West (died young)
Henry Clay West (died young)
Oscar Dunreath West (1840, died in the Civil War)
Richard James West (1843–1886)
William Newton West (born 1847)
Nancy Woodson West
Amelia Putnam West

Maleta West
Born: March 26, 1812, Kentucky
Died: September 28, 1880
Married: Nathaniel Ector Harrelson, September 6, 1831
Children: Amanda Harrelson (born 1834)
James West Harrelson (born 1836)
William Howard Harrelson (born 1840)
John Bracken Harrelson (born 1847)

Alinda West
Born: August 1, 1813, Kentucky
Died: November 12, 1866, Pleasant Hill, Missouri
Married: William Warlock Wright
H. M. Bracken
Children: Marion Wallas Wright (born 1843)

Silas Mercer West
Born: January 27, 1817, Kentucky
Died: Date unknown
Married: Not known
Children: James West
Six daughters

Elias Putnam West
  Born: March 14, 1820, Kentucky
  Died: January 26, 1892, Lawrence, Kansas
  Known children: Alice Webster West
                        Maria Louisa West
                        Toby Putnam West

William Newton West
  Born: January 19, 1821, Kentucky
  Died: 1863, Arkansas
  Married: Joyce Powell, 1851
  Children: Mary Susan West (born 1853)

Mary West
  Born: September 3, 1823, Kentucky
  Died: Date unknown, Harrisonville, Missouri
  Married: Williams
  Children: Four

James Leland West
  Born: September 3, 1826, Kentucky
  Died: Date unknown, Fayetteville, Arkansas
  Married: A widow in Arkansas
  Children: Howard West
                 Two daughters

TILLMAN HOWARD WEST

Tillman Howard West received his middle name from his mother's Howard family. Not only did Tillman's father marry a Howard, Mary Mourning, but also his uncle John West married Mary Mourning's sister, Lavenia Jane Howard. Mary Mourning Howard was born on July 14, 1784 in South Carolina. She was the daughter of Amelia Putnam Howard. Mary Mourning Howard West, Tillman's mother, died in Simpson County, Kentucky in 1869.

Tillman Howard West married Elizabeth James, who was a sister of Robert Sallee James, the father of Frank, Jesse, and Susan James. Jesse James was known to use several aliases during his career, but the one he used most was Howard. During his years in Nashville, Tennessee, Jesse used the name J. D. (James or John Davis) Howard. At the time of his death in 1882, he was living in St. Joseph, Missouri under the name of Tom Howard. It is, therefore, apparent that Jesse James took his favorite alias from the family of his Uncle Tillman's mother.

Tillman and his wife, Elizabeth James West, moved from Logan County, Kentucky in 1844 to Pleasant Hill, Missouri. Tillman served as postmaster in Clay County, Missouri in 1847. Tillman later moved to Randolph, Missouri and then to Harlem, Missouri, where he operated a hotel and engaged in buying land from the government in Clay and Jackson counties in Missouri.

Crossing the river, Tillman built a general merchandise store along the banks of the Missouri river. His store along the levee became known as Westport Landing, which became the first name for Kansas City, as the city became established. Tillman also owned and operated a large grist mill at Blue Springs, Missouri. He closed his business enterprises during the Civil War, but at the war's end Tillman and his two sons, Richard and William, established Kansas City's largest men's clothing store. Tillman and his wife,

Elizabeth, helped organize and were charter members of the Methodist Episcopal Church South in Kansas City, and at the time of her death in 1904, Elizabeth was the oldest member of this church.

Tillman died in Kansas City on October 3, 1884, and his wife, Elizabeth James West, died at Mountain Grove, Missouri on November 2, 1904. Both are buried in the Kansas City Union Cemetery.

Jesse and Frank James resided in this Nashville, Tennessee home with their families from 1878-1881. (Photo courtesy of Ted Yeatman.)

CHAPTER 6

The
Tennessee
James Family

Studying the family history of Jesse and Frank James is made somewhat confusing by the fact that another James line appears with children also named Jesse and Frank James, near the same ages as their distant cousins, Jesse and Frank from Missouri. Since the Jesse and Frank James who were born in Tennessee apparently were also often on the outlaw trail and since the noted Missouri bandits Jesse and Frank James were known to spend considerable time around Nashville, Tennessee, there is even greater confusion. Family stories from the Tennessee James family indicate that Jesse and Frank did often visit Dr. Aaron James at his home on Yellow Creek in Dickson County, Tennessee. According to the Tennessee records, Dr. Aaron James's great-uncle, Thomas James, was a brother of William James, who was the great-grandfather of Jesse and Frank James, the Missouri outlaws. Because the relationship was so distant, it is this writer's opinion that it is very doubtful that Jesse and Frank James were even aware of their relationship to the Tennessee Jameses. Jesse and Frank James of Missouri chose the Nashville region as a safe location to elude the law for reasons other than that they had distant relatives there. As for the reports that they visited Dr. Aaron James, they could be true, as the man was a noted physician in

Jesse James, using the alias J. D. Howard, lived in this home in Nashville, Tennessee for several years.

the region and could have respected their anonymity if indeed he knew about the relationship. What we know of this Tennessee James family is as follows:

John James
    Born: Pembrokeshire, Wales
    Died: 1726, Bucks County, Pennsylvania
    Known children: Thomas
                    William James

Thomas James[1]
    Born: Date unknown
    Died: circa 1775
    Married: Not known
    Known children: Samuel James
                    James James
                    Josiah James
                    Isaac James

Aaron James (born 1775)
William James (1754–1805)

Aaron James
 Born: 1755, Bucks County, Pennsylvania
 Died: Dickson County, Tennessee
 Married: Not known
 Known children: Enos James

Enos James
 Born: Date unknown, Dickson County,
  Tennessee
 Died: Date unknown, Dickson County,
  Tennessee
 Married: Not known
 Children: Aaron James (1820–1896)
  Areua Perigen
  Frank James
  Dudley James
  Charles James
  Thomas James
  John James
  Betsy James
  Jesse James

Aaron James, son of Enos, was born in Dickson County, Tennessee along Yellow Creek in 1820. He married Elizabeth Holt. Aaron attended the Louisville

1. According to Tennessee James family records, William and Thomas James were children of John James. These records further indicate William was the great-grandfather of Jesse and Frank James, and his brother Thomas founded the Tennessee James family. Such Tennessee family records are recorded in old family Bibles, but have not been fully documented.

Medical College in Kentucky. In 1849, he attended the Nashville, Tennessee Medical College, where he met his wife, Elizabeth. In 1860 Dr. James acquired a farm near the Crowell, Tennessee, community, now Poplar Grove, along Tumbling Creek in Humphreys County, Tennessee. There he provided medical services to both Federal and Confederate forces throughout the Civil War.

Dr. Aaron's daughter Lulu married a man named Hudgens. Nothing more is known about her.

Ida Penelope James married John Marshall Smith.

Enos Hardeman James
   Born: October 2, 1854
   Died: January 11, 1906
   Married: N. E. James
   Children: Charles Edward James (1877–1939)
              Richard James (1879–1973)
              John James (1882–1936)
              Jesse James (1884–1972)
              Dorris James (born 1888)
              Etta James (1891–1969)
              Lulu James (1893–1978)
              Leonard Dudley James (1895–1979)
              James Coleman (born 1897)

Charles Edward James was born on June 29, 1877 and died on October 15, 1939 near Poplar Grove, Tennessee. He married Evie Beasley. Their children were Burton Elam James, born 1904; Charles Harold James, born 1909; Aenos Randolph James, born 1912; Ralph James, born 1917; Raleigh James, born 1923; and Kathryn James, born 1914, who married Pherie Rodgers.

Richard James, son of Enos Hardeman, was last known living in Miami, Florida with his wife, Kate

Mr. and Mrs. James (Jesse) Coleman James, 1984, Old Hickory, Tennessee. (Photo by author.)

Nance. Their children are Leland and Alois James.

John James, born December 6, 1882, married Roas Sanders and lived near Poplar Grove, Tennessee. Their known children are Marvin, Edith, Mildred, Burnice, Margaret, Sanders, Ray, Herbert, and Buford James.

Jesse James was born June 22, 1884 and lived in Waverly, Tennessee. Jesse married Beulah Richard. Their known children were Willie, Annie, Frank, Pearl Bee, Earl Dee, Emma, and Debert Hardiman James.

Dorris James, born June 15, 1888, married Ester Stage and resided near Poplar Grove, Tennessee. Their known children were Olisie, Eugenia, Roland, Warren, Leon, Beunard, and Bobby.

Etta B. James was born September 3, 1891 and married Jim Stringer. They lived in Greenville, Tennessee.

Lulu James was born December 3, 1893 and married Harvey Jenkins. They resided at Poplar Grove, Tennessee. Their two known children were Keith and Paul Jenkins.

Leonard Dudley James was born April 12, 1895. Dudley married Alice Stage. They also lived in the Poplar Grove, Tennessee community, and their known children were Audrey and Claude James.

James Coleman James, the youngest child of Enos Hardeman James, was born April 3, 1897. Known as Jesse James around the Old Hickory, Tennessee community, he provided this writer with this history of the Tennessee James family in 1985. James Coleman married Mary Ethel Stringer, who was born March 18, 1899. James and his wife have the following children: Elsie Lou (Parrott), Grady Carl James, Edna Marie (Madden), Edsel Ford James, Donna (Hardeman), John Edward, Gene Richard, Jimmy Coleman, Jr., Loyd, and Floyd James.

CHAPTER 7

The
Ford
Family

The decision to include a portion on the Ford family in this James family study was a difficult one. Many past writers on the James brothers have mistakenly suggested that Jesse James was killed by his cousin Bob Ford. Just where such writers got the impression Bob and Charlie Ford were related to Jesse James is not known. A thorough study of the James and Ford families has not turned up any possible family relationship between them. The reader should, therefore, not interpret the inclusion of the Ford family as a suggestion that there may have been a family relationship.

Because of Bob Ford's assassination of Jesse James and because of his brother Charlie's involvement in the plot, what is currently known of the Ford family is included here. Though it is not nearly as popular as trying to prove a family connection with the James brothers, hundreds of people also seek a family relationship with Jesse's assassin. This writer has received numerous inquiries regarding the Ford family, and the James Farm has many visitors each year making inquiries of the Fords. What is currently known of this family is as follows:

Austin Ford
    Born: 1790, Fauquier County, Virginia

Robert Newton Ford. He shot Jesse James on April 3, 1882 in St. Joseph, Missouri.

Died: July, 1841
Married: Jane Allison (1817 or 1818)

Austin Ford met his wife, Jane Allison, while he was serving in the military and was active in campaigns against the Indians in Florida. Jane was born in Florida in 1794. Austin returned to Fauquier County, Virginia after his marriage and practiced his trade as a stonemason. Austin and Jane Allison had the following known children in Virginia:

James Thomas Ford (born 1820)
John W. Ford
Lucella Ford
Charles Ford (born 1828)

Elizabeth Ford
Mary Jane Ford
William H. Ford
Arthur F. Ford (died 1885)
Robert A. Ford (born March 13, 1840)

In 1840, Austin took his family from Virginia to Clark County, Missouri, where he managed a large farm for a man named Lee. In July of 1841, Ford was killed from a blow to the head in an altercation with Lee. John Wesley Ford then became head of the household. John married Anna Maria Storey and operated Seybolts Tavern in Missouri in 1870. John and Maria's children were William Ezra, Mary Jane, Georginia, John H., Edwin, Luther, and Florida. Georginia and Florida died as children. Austin Ford's widow, Jane Allison, moved to Clay County, Missouri in 1851, where she died in 1857.

Charles Ford married a girl from Tennessee named

The home in St. Joseph, Missouri where Jesse James, using the alias Tom Howard, was living with his wife and children when he was killed by Bob Ford on April 3, 1882.

Martha and spent his life as a farmer near Richmond in Ray County, Missouri.

Robert Austin Ford was born in Virginia on March 13, 1840. He married Mary E. Story, a daughter of Thomas and Luck A. (Baldwin) Story in Clay County, Missouri. Luck was born in Clay County in 1850. Robert A. and Mary had the following children: Oscar A., John T., Jesse James, Ella T., Walter N., Maggie L., Robert A., Flora Belle, and Arthur F. The following children all died young: John T., Flora, and Arthur.

James Thomas Ford was born in Virginia in 1820. He married Mary Ann Bruin, daughter of Elias and Ann Bruin, in Virginia on August 10, 1840. James moved to Missouri along with his father, Austin, and their family. James T. Ford returned to Virginia shortly after his father died and there became a tenant farmer for John A. Washington at Mt. Vernon. In 1843, James T. and his wife returned to Clark County, Missouri, where the following children were born:

This photo of Jesse James was taken the day after he was killed. The wound on his left temple is clearly noticeable. (Photo courtesy of St. Joseph Museum.)

Ed O'Kelley, who killed Bob Ford in Creede, Colorado, June 8, 1892.

Georgia Ford (born 1844)
John T. Ford (born 1846)
Elias Capline Ford
Martha and Amanda Ford (twins—born 1855)
Charles Wilson Ford (born July 9, 1857)
Wilber Ford (born 1860)
Robert Newton Ford (born January 31, 1862)

Shortly after Robert Newton Ford was born, the family returned to Mt. Vernon for a short period before finally settling on a farm in Clay County, Missouri. A well-known student of the Bible, James Thomas pastored a church near their home.

William H. Ford married Artella Cummins on September 21, 1862 and later Amanda Goode on February 27, 1866. William lived near Kearney, Missouri, where his children Fanny and Albert Ford were born.

The last home of Jesse James as it appeared a few hours after Jesse was killed by Bob Ford, April 3, 1882. (Photo courtesy Pony Express Historical Association, St. Joseph, Missouri.)

The home where Jesse James was killed as it appears today in St. Joseph, Missouri. It is operated by the Pony Express Historical Association. (Photo courtesy of the author.)

Charles Wilson Ford, the fifth child of James Thomas Ford and Mary (Bruin) Ford, was born on July 9, 1857. Charles had apparently been involved with the James-Younger gang and was accepted by Jesse James. Charles went to St. Joseph some months before April 3, 1882, and because he was wanted by the law he was staying in Jesse's home. While they were planning the robbery of a Platte City, Nebraska bank, Charles Ford persuaded Jesse James to let his younger brother, Bob Ford, age twenty, participate. When Bob arrived at Jesse's St. Joseph, Missouri home, Charles and Bob carefully waited for the proper moment to carry out the plot they had previously arranged with Missouri Governor Crittenden and law officials to bring down the notorious Jesse James. After breakfast on the morning of April 3, 1882, Jesse, Bob, and Charles left the kitchen and entered the parlor. Jesse removed his gun belt and laid it on a day bed. Noticing a picture on the wall that needed straightening or dusting, he stood on a chair. At that moment Robert Newton Ford fired his .44 and Jesse James fell dead.

Charles Ford became distraught over the tremendous public ridicule he and his brother received over shooting the famous, unarmed outlaw Jesse James in the back of the head. Charles committed suicide on May 6, 1884, two years after their cowardly deed.

Bob Ford, apparently with a good portion of reward money, journeyed to Creede, Colorado where he established a saloon and reveled in the notoriety he had earned as the man who killed Jesse James. A man named O'Kelley, apparently a fan of Jesse James, became inebriated and walked into Ford's saloon and shot and killed him on June 8, 1892. Buried in Colorado, Ford's body was exhumed a few years later by his family and returned to Missouri.

WILLIAM JAMES
(1754–1805)

JOHN JAMES (1775–1827)

NANCY ANN JAMES (HODGES)

(1777)

MARY JAMES (LEE)

WILLIAM JAMES, JR. (1782–1807)

RICHARD JAMES

THOMAS JAMES (1783)

MARTIN JAMES (1789–1867)

JOHN JAMES

- MARY JAMES (MIMMS) (1809–1877)
- WILLIAM JAMES (1811–1895)
- JOHN R. JAMES (1815–1887)
- ELIZABETH JAMES (WEST) (1816–1904)
- ROBERT SALLEE JAMES (1818–1850)
- NANCY GARDNER JAMES (HITE) (1821–1875)
- THOMAS MARTIN JAMES (1823–1903)
- DRURY WOODSON JAMES (1826–1910)

ROBERT SALLEE JAMES
(1818–1850)

ALEXANDER FRANKLIN JAMES
(1843–1915)

ROBERT R. JAMES (1845, died as an
infant)

JESSE WOODSON JAMES (1847–
1882)

SUSAN LAVENIA JAMES (1849–
1889)

ALEXANDER FRANKLIN JAMES

ROBERT FRANKLIN JAMES (1878–
1959)

JESSE WOODSON JAMES

JESSE EDWARDS JAMES (1875–1951)

TWINS: GOULD and

MONTGOMERY JAMES (died as infants)

MARY SUSAN JAMES (1879–1935)

SUSAN LAVENIA JAMES (PARMER)

ROBERT ARCHIE PARMER (1872–1883)

FLORA PARMER (BENSON) (1877–1926)

ZELMA PARMER (EDWARDS) (1879–1972)

ALLEN PARMER, JR. (1882–1885)

SUSAN KATE PARMER (1885–1903)

FETA PARMER (ROSE)(1887–1978)

JESSE EDWARDS JAMES

LUCILLE MARTHA JAMES (LEWIS)
(1900-1988)

JOSEPHINE FRANCIS JAMES (ROSS)
(1902-1964)

JESSIE ESTELLE JAMES (BAUMEL)
(1906-1987)

ETHEL ROSE JAMES (OWENS)
(born 1908)

MARY SUSAN JAMES
(BARR)

LAWRENCE H. BARR (1902–1984)

FORSTER RAY BARR (1904–1977)

CHESTER A. BARR (1907–1984)

HENRIETTA BARR (1913, died an infant)

Index